Less Fret

more Faith

AN 11-WEEK ACTION PLAN
TO **OVERCOME ANXIETY**

Max Lucado

Thomas Nelson
Since 1798

Published in Nashville, Tennessee, by Thomas Nelson. Thomas Nelson is a registered trademark of HarperCollins Christian Publishing, Inc.

Thomas Nelson titles may be purchased in bulk for educational, business, fund-raising, or sales promotional use. For information, please e-mail SpecialMarkets@ThomasNelson.com.

Unless otherwise noted, Scripture quotations are taken from the New King James Version®. © 1982 by Thomas Nelson. Used by permission. All rights reserved.

Scripture quotations marked ASV are from the Authorized Standard Version. Public domain.

Scripture quotations marked THE MESSAGE are from *The Message*. Copyright © by Eugene H. Peterson 1993, 1994, 1995, 1996, 2000, 2001, 2002. Used by permission of NavPress. All rights reserved. Represented by Tyndale House Publishers, Inc.

Scripture quotations marked NCV are from the New Century Version®. © 2005 by Thomas Nelson. Used by permission. All rights reserved.

Scripture quotations marked NIV are from the Holy Bible, New International Version®, NIV®. Copyright © 1973, 1978, 1984, 2011 by Biblica, Inc.® Used by permission of Zondervan. All rights reserved worldwide. www.Zondervan.com. The "NIV" and "New International Version" are trademarks registered in the United States Patent and Trademark Office by Biblica, Inc.®

Scripture quotations marked NLT are from the Holy Bible, New Living Translation. © 1996, 2004, 2007, 2013, 2015 by Tyndale House Foundation. Used by permission of Tyndale House Publishers, Inc., Carol Stream, Illinois 60188. All rights reserved.

Scripture quotations marked RSV are from Revised Standard Version of the Bible. Copyright 1946, 1952, and 1971 National Council of the Churches of Christ in the United States of America. Used by permission. All rights reserved.

ISBN 978-1-4002-0748-0 (eBook)
ISBN 978-1-4002-0749-7 (SC)

Printed in the United States of America
19 20 21 LSC 15 14 13 12

CONTENTS

Introduction

ANXIOUS FOR NOTHING

It's a low-grade fear. An edginess, a dread. A cold wind that won't stop howling.

It's not so much a storm as the certainty that one is coming. Always . . . coming. Sunny days are just an interlude. You can't relax. Can't let your guard down. All peace is temporary, short-term.

It's not the sight of a grizzly but the suspicion of one or two or ten. Behind every tree. Beyond every turn. Inevitable. It's just a matter of time until the grizzly leaps out of the shadows, bares its fangs, and gobbles you up, along with your family, your friends, your bank account, your pets, and your country.

There's trouble out there! So you don't sleep well.

You don't laugh often.

You don't enjoy the sun.

You don't whistle as you walk.

And when others do, you give them a look. *That* look. That "are you naïve?" look. You may even give them a word. "Haven't you read the news and heard the reports and seen the studies?"

Airplanes fall out of the sky. Bull markets go bear. Terrorists terrorize. Good people turn bad. The other shoe will drop. Fine print will be found. Misfortune lurks out there; it's just a matter of time.

Anxiety is a meteor shower of what-ifs. What if I don't close the sale? What if we don't get the bonus? What if we can't afford braces for the kids? What if my kids have crooked teeth? What if crooked teeth keep them from having friends, a career, or a spouse? What if they end up homeless and hungry, holding a cardboard sign that reads: "My parents couldn't afford braces for me"?

Anxiety is trepidation.

It's a suspicion, an apprehension. Life in a minor key with major concerns. Perpetually on the pirate ship's plank.

You're part Chicken Little and part Eeyore. The sky is falling, and it's falling disproportionately on you.

As a result you are anxious. A free-floating sense of dread hovers over you, a caul across the heart, a nebulous hunch about things . . . that might happen . . . sometime in the future.

Anxiety and fear are cousins but not twins. Fear sees a threat. Anxiety imagines one.

Fear screams, *Get out!*

Anxiety ponders, *What if?*

Fear results in fight or flight. Anxiety creates doom and gloom. Fear is the pulse that pounds when you see a coiled rattlesnake in your front yard. Anxiety is the voice that tells you, *Never, ever, for the rest of your life, walk barefooted through the grass. There might be a snake . . . somewhere.*

The word *anxious* defines itself. It is a hybrid of *angst* and *xious*. *Angst* is a sense of unease. *Xious* is the sound I make on the tenth step of a flight of stairs when my heart beats fast and I run low on oxygen. I can be heard inhaling and exhaling, sounding like the second syllable of *anxious*, which makes me wonder if anxious people aren't just that: people who are out of breath because of the angst of life.

A native Hawaiian once told me the origin of the name that islanders use for us non-Hawaiians—*haole*. *Haole* is a Hawaiian word for "no breath." The name became associated with the European immigrants of the 1820s.[1] While there are varying explanations for this term, I like the one he gave me: "Our forefathers thought the settlers were always in a hurry to build plantations, harbors, and ranches. To the native Hawaiians they seemed short of breath."

Anxiety takes our breath, for sure. If only that were all it took. It also takes our sleep. Our energy. Our well-being. "Do not fret," wrote the psalmist, "it only causes harm" (Ps. 37:8). Harm to our necks, jaws, backs, and bowels. Anxiety can twist us into emotional pretzels. It can make our eyes twitch, blood pressure rise, heads ache, and armpits sweat. To see the consequences of anxiety, just read about half the ailments in a medical textbook.

Anxiety ain't fun.

Chances are that you or someone you know seriously struggles with anxiety. According to the National Institute of Mental Health, anxiety disorders are reaching epidemic proportions. In a given year nearly fifty million Americans will feel the effects of a panic attack, phobias, or other anxiety disorders. Our chests will tighten. We'll feel dizzy and light-headed. We'll fear crowds and avoid people. Anxiety disorders in the United States are the "number one mental health problem among . . . women and are second only to alcohol and drug abuse among men."[2]

"The United States is now the most anxious

nation in the world."[3] (Congratulations to us!) The land of the Stars and Stripes has become the country of stress and strife. This is a costly achievement. "Stress-related ailments cost the nation $300 billion every year in medical bills and lost productivity, while our usage of sedative drugs keeps skyrocketing; just between 1997 and 2004, Americans more than doubled their spending on anti-anxiety medications like Xanax and Valium, from $900 million to $2.1 billion."[4] The *Journal of the American Medical Association* cited a study that indicates an exponential increase in depression. People of each generation in the twentieth century "were three times more likely to experience depression" than people of the preceding generation.[5]

How can this be? Our cars are safer than ever. We regulate food and water and electricity. Though gangs still prowl our streets, most Americans do not live under the danger of imminent attack. Yet if worry were an Olympic event, we'd win the gold medal!

Citizens in other countries ironically enjoy

more tranquility. They experience one-fifth the anxiety levels of Americans, despite having fewer of the basic life necessities. "What's more, when these less-anxious developing-world citizens immigrate to the United States, they tend to get just as anxious as Americans. Something about our particular way of life, then, is making us less calm and composed."[6]

Our college kids are feeling it as well. In a study that involved more than two hundred thousand incoming freshmen, "students reported all-time lows in overall mental health and emotional stability."[7] As psychologist Robert Leahy points out, "The average *child* today exhibits the same level of anxiety as the average *psychiatric patient* in the 1950s."[8] Kids have more toys, clothes, and opportunities than ever, but by the time they leave home, they are wrapped tighter than Egyptian mummies.

We are tense.

Why? What is the cause of our anxiety?

Change, for one thing. Researchers speculate that the Western world's "environment and social order have changed more in the last thirty years than they have in the previous three hundred"![9] Think what has changed. Technology. The existence of the Internet. Increased warnings about global warming, nuclear war, and terrorist attacks. Changes and new threats are imported into our lives every few seconds thanks to smartphones, TVs, and computer screens. In our grandparents' generation news of an earthquake in Nepal would reach around the world some days later. In our parents' day the nightly news communicated the catastrophe. Now it is a matter of minutes. We've barely processed one crisis, and then we hear of another.

In addition we move faster than ever before. Our ancestors traveled as far as a horse or camel could take them during daylight. But us? We jet through time zones as if they were neighborhood streets. Our great-grandparents had to turn down the brain sensors when the sun set. But us? We turn on the cable news, open the laptop, or tune in to the latest survival show.

For years I kept a nightly appointment with the ten o'clock news. Nothing like falling to sleep with the accounts of murders and catastrophes fresh on the brain.

And what about the onslaught of personal challenges? You or someone you know is facing foreclosure, fighting cancer, slugging through a divorce, or battling addiction. You or someone you know is bankrupt, broke, or going out of business.

Without exception we are getting older. And with age comes a covey of changes. My wife found an app that guesses a person's age by evaluating a picture of the person's face. It missed Denalyn's age by fifteen years to the young side. She liked that. It missed mine by five years to the old side. So I retook it. It added seven more. Then ten. I quit before it pronounced me dead.

One would think Christians would be exempt from worry. But we are not. We have been taught that the Christian life is a life of peace, and when we don't have peace, we assume the problem lies within us. Not only do we feel anxious, but we also feel guilty about our anxiety! The result is a downward spiral of worry, guilt, worry, guilt.

It's enough to cause a person to get anxious.

It's enough to make us wonder if the apostle Paul was out of touch with reality when he wrote, "Be anxious for nothing" (Phil. 4:6).

"Be anxious for less" would have been a sufficient challenge. Or "Be anxious only on Thursdays." Or "Be anxious only in seasons of severe affliction."

But Paul doesn't seem to offer any leeway here. Be anxious for nothing. Nada. Zilch. Zero. Is this what he meant? Not exactly. He wrote the phrase in the present active tense, which implies an ongoing state. It's the life of *perpetual anxiety* that Paul wanted to address. The *Lucado Revised Translation* reads, "Don't let anything in life leave you perpetually breathless and in angst." The presence of anxiety is unavoidable, but the prison of anxiety is optional.

Anxiety is not a sin; it is an emotion. (So

don't be anxious about feeling anxious.) Anxiety can, however, lead to sinful behavior. When we numb our fears with six-packs or food binges, when we spew anger like Krakatau, when we peddle our fears to anyone who will buy them, we are sinning. If toxic anxiety leads you to abandon your spouse, neglect your kids, break covenants, or break hearts, take heed. Jesus gave this word: "Be careful, or your hearts will be weighed down with . . . the anxieties of life" (Luke 21:34 NIV). Is your heart weighed down with worry?

Look for these signals:

- Are you laughing less than you once did?
- Do you see problems in every promise?
- Would those who know you best describe you as increasingly negative and critical?
- Do you assume that something bad is going to happen?
- Do you dilute and downplay good news with doses of your version of reality?

- Many days would you rather stay in bed than get up?
- Do you magnify the negative and dismiss the positive?
- Given the chance, would you avoid any interaction with humanity for the rest of your life?

If you answered yes to most of these questions, I have a friend for you to meet. Actually, I have a scripture for you to read. I've read the words so often that we have become friends. I'd like to nominate this passage for the Scripture Hall of Fame. The museum wall that contains the framed words of the Twenty-third Psalm, the Lord's Prayer, and John 3:16 should also display Philippians 4:4–8:

> Rejoice in the Lord always. Again I will say, rejoice! Let your gentleness be known to all men. The Lord is at hand. Be anxious for nothing, but in everything by prayer and supplication, with thanksgiving, let your

requests be made known to God; and the
peace of God, which surpasses all understanding, will guard your hearts and minds
through Christ Jesus. Finally, brethren,
whatever things are true, whatever things
are noble, whatever things are just, whatever things are pure, whatever things are
lovely, whatever things are of good report,
if there is any virtue and if there is anything
praiseworthy—meditate on these things.

Five verses with four admonitions that lead
to one wonderful promise: "the peace of God,
which surpasses all understanding, will guard
your hearts and minds" (v. 7).

Celebrate God's goodness. "Rejoice in the
Lord always" (v. 4).

Ask God for help. "Let your requests be
made known to God" (v. 6).

Leave your concerns with him. "With
thanksgiving . . ." (v. 6).

Meditate on good things. "Think about the things that are good and worthy of praise" (v. 8 NCV).

Celebrate. Ask. Leave. Meditate.

C.A.L.M.

Could you use some calm? If so, you aren't alone. The Bible is Kindle's most highlighted book. And Philippians 4:6–7 is the most highlighted passage.[10] Apparently we all could use a word of comfort.

God is ready to give it.

With God as your helper, you will sleep better tonight and smile more tomorrow. You'll reframe the way you face your fears. You'll learn how to talk yourself off the ledge, view bad news through the lens of sovereignty, discern the lies of Satan, and tell yourself the truth.

You will discover a life that is characterized by calm and will develop tools for facing the onslaughts of anxiety. It will require some work on your part. I certainly don't mean to leave the impression that anxiety can be waved away with a simple pep talk. In fact, for some of you God's healing will include the help of therapy and/or medication. If that is the case, do not for a moment think that you are a second-class citizen of heaven. Ask God to lead you to a qualified counselor or physician who will provide the treatment you need.

This much is sure: It is not God's will that you lead a life of perpetual anxiety. It is not his will that you face every day with dread and trepidation. He made you for more than a life of breath-stealing angst and mind-splitting worry. He has a new chapter for your life. And he is ready to write it.

I have a childhood memory that I cherish. My father loved corn bread and buttermilk. (Can you guess that I was raised in a small West Texas town?) About ten o'clock each night he would meander into the kitchen and crumble a piece of corn bread into a glass of buttermilk. He would stand at the counter in his T-shirt and boxer shorts and drink it.

He then made the rounds to the front and back doors, checking the locks. Once everything was secure, he would step into the bedroom I shared with my brother and say something like, "Everything is secure, boys. You can go to sleep now."

I have no inclination to believe that God loves corn bread and buttermilk, but I do believe he loves his children. He oversees your world. He monitors your life. He doesn't need to check the doors; indeed, he is the door. Nothing will come your way apart from his permission.

Listen carefully and you will hear him say, "Everything is secure. You can rest now." By his power you will "be anxious for nothing" and discover the "peace . . . which passes all understanding" (RSV).

Dear Lord,

You spoke to storms. Would you speak to ours? You calmed the hearts of the apostles. Would you calm the chaos within us? You told them to fear not. Say the same to us. We are weary from our worry, battered and belittled by the gales of life. Oh Prince of Peace, bequeath to us a spirit of calm.

As we turn the page in this book, will you turn a new leaf in our lives? Quench anxiety. Stir courage. Let us know less fret and more faith.

In your name, amen.

ASSESS YOUR TOOL KIT

Whether we know it or not, we all have coping strategies. We have a tool kit to open in times of anxiety. Some tools are healthy, others counterproductive. An important step in assembling good tools is identifying the bad ones. Examine the list below, and place a check next to the tools you use.

When I am anxious, I do the following:

___ try to relax
___ seek advice and assurance from a
    trusted friend
___ take prescription medication

___ suppress my feelings

___ busy myself with activities unrelated to my problem (e.g., wash clothes, mow the grass)

___ get angry

___ have a smoke

___ pray, meditate, read Scripture

___ try to understand the source of my worry

___ other _____

Evaluate your list. Are your coping methods, by and large, good ones? Or does your response to anxiety create even more problems? Reduce your list to the tools that actually help you resolve the problem. Share your revised list with someone you trust, and ask that person to pray with you about a new strategy.

VERSE FOR REFLECTION

Every good gift and every perfect gift is from above, and comes down from the Father of lights, with whom there is no variation or shadow of turning. (James 1:17)

Pray It Through

Lord,

Grant me the wisdom to remember that you are not the source of anxiety. Rather, help me remember that resting in you provides relief from all worry. Give me the courage to choose what is good and pure, even when it is hard or inconvenient.

In your holy name, amen.

Week 2

EVALUATE YOUR
WORRY PATTERNS

This week make a note every time you feel anxious. Observe some details about your troubling thoughts.

- What were you worried about? Here are some examples to get you thinking.
  "This traffic will make me late for the meeting! I'm going to miss the best part!"
  "I'm worried that it's going to rain on next Saturday's picnic."

"I catch myself thinking about the kids
and their college tuition. Are we
saving enough money?"

- What situation or event triggered the
anxiety?
- How did this anxiety make you feel?
- How did you react?

Take a few minutes to review what you have
observed about your worries.

- Try to identify the core fear or
insecurity behind the anxiety. Do you
see a common theme? Is there some
catastrophic event you fear?
- How many of your worries
materialized? Highlight the number
of times you were worried about
something that never actually
happened.
- Was the gain worth the pain? As you
look at the emotional toll the anxiety
took, was it worth it?

- How did your anxiety affect others in your life?
- Is there anything you can do to address the source of anxiety? What is a practical step you can take? Make an intentional choice to act so the next time this anxiety surfaces, you can tell yourself what you are doing to alleviate the potential problem.

Each morning add your concern to your prayer time. Ask God to go ahead of you.

Verse for Reflection

And we know that all things work together for good to those who love God, to those who are the called according to His purpose. (Rom. 8:28)

Pray It Through

Father,

I release the fears and anxieties I face today, and I place them in your hands. Help me surrender my tendency to try to control certainty. May the truth that you are sovereign over every detail of today bring peace to my heart and my mind.

In Jesus' name, amen.

Week 3

CLEAN YOUR
LIFE LENS

Everyone has assumptions about life. Many are useful and constructive. We know that the sun will rise and set each day. We assume that storms will pass and that food will be available in grocery stores. Some assumptions, however, are toxic. Even worse, they are contrary to the truth. Unhealthy assumptions include thoughts like these:

> *I'm unworthy.* I don't deserve to have good things happen to me.

People abandon me. When people come to
know the real me, they leave.
It's all my fault. I'm to blame for every bad
thing that happens to me.
*No one has my back, which makes me
vulnerable.* Something bad is going to
happen.
The world feels dangerous. I'm scared.

Many false beliefs were formed in the early
years of our lives when we did not have the abil-
ity to challenge them. So their roots run deep,
and such false assumptions create an anxiety-
ridden life. God's solution? Truth. Face worries
with truth. Bring "every thought into captivity
to the obedience of Christ" (2 Cor. 10:5 ASV).
One way to do this is to correct faulty thinking
with accurate thoughts.

I matter to God. He made me, knows me,
and has a plan for my life.
I am worthy of love. I'm not perfect, but I
have abilities and God-given gifts.

9

I'm not responsible for all the bad things.
I've made mistakes, but I am learning
and growing, and, most of all, I am
forgiven by God.

I'm protected. It is a dangerous world, but
I serve a mighty God who knows and
loves me.

Listen to yourself. Monitor your beliefs
about yourself, about God, and about the world.
Don't allow false assumptions to take up any
space in your mind. Immediately treat them
with truth.

Verse for Reflection

Consider the ravens: They do not sow or reap,
they have no storeroom or barn; yet God feeds
them. And how much more valuable you are
than birds! Who of you by worrying can add
a single hour to your life? Since you cannot do
this very little thing, why do you worry about
the rest? (Luke 12:24–26 NIV)

PRAY IT THROUGH

Lord,

Deconstruct the lies I believe about myself, about the world, and about you. Replace those lies with the truth of your love and care. Help me get out of the way. Please re-create my perspective so that truth reigns and guides my beliefs, decisions, and actions.

In your holy name, amen.

Week 4

CAST A VOTE IN
YOUR FAVOR

You are either your worst critic or greatest cheerleader. Either you tear yourself down or you build yourself up. The words you tell yourself can usher in fear or faith. Are you against you? Or are you for you?

God is for you. "If God is for us, who can be against us?" (Rom. 8:31). He has cast his vote. In his opinion you are worth the death of his Son. You are valuable, purposeful, and important. "Fear not, for I have redeemed you; I have called you by name, you are mine" (Isa. 43:1 RSV).

If God is for you, shouldn't you be for you? Does it make sense for you to be against you? You are against you when you call yourself dumb, ugly, or poor. You are against you when you tell yourself there is no solution, hope, or promise in life. You are against you when you decide you have no talents or friends or future.

The words you tell yourself have power. If you tell yourself something often enough, guess what? It becomes your version of the truth! Those offhand negative remarks you mumble about yourself aren't harmless; they are toxic. They actually agree with the devil. They give him a foothold. "The soothing tongue is a tree of life, but a perverse tongue crushes the spirit" (Prov. 15:4 NIV).

Hold fast to the promises of Scripture. Tell yourself the truth about yourself. The apostle Paul modeled this for us. "No, in all these things we are more than conquerors through him who loved us. For I am convinced that neither death nor life, neither angels nor demons, neither the present nor the future, nor any powers, neither height nor depth, nor anything else in all creation, will be able to separate us from the love of God that is in Christ Jesus our Lord" (Rom. 8:37–39 NIV).

Personalize that passage. Insert the sources of anxiety that come your way. "No, in all these things we are more than conquerors through him who loved us. For I am convinced that neither *poor health* nor *poor decisions*, neither *college debt* nor *pink slips*, neither *today's deadline* nor *tomorrow's diagnosis*, nor any *job transfers*, neither *addictions* nor *moral failures*, nor anything else in all creation, will be able to separate me from the love of God that is in Christ Jesus our Lord."

Be for you! God is.

VERSE FOR REFLECTION

Use Romans 8:37–39 as quoted above.

Pray It Through

Lord,

Make my tongue a tree of life! Help me see myself and my situation in light of what you have done for me. Keep your love for me in the forefront of my mind today.

In your precious name, amen.

Week 5

CATCH YOUR
BREATH

Time for rest must be taken daily and weekly. God told Moses, "Six days do your work, but on the seventh day do not work, so that your ox and your donkey may rest, and so that the slave born in your household and the foreigner living among you may be refreshed" (Ex. 23:12 NIV).

This was not a suggestion, recommendation, or piece of practical advice. This was a command. Rest! Once a week let the system reboot. Once a week let the entire household slow down. The Israelite who violated this law paid for the sin with his or her life. Today the death penalty is still in effect, but the death is a gradual one that comes from overwork, stress, and anxiety.

The Bible does not see rest as a sign of weakness or laziness but as a mark of reverence. To observe a Sabbath day of rest is to announce, "God knows what I need more than I do. If he says to rest, I will rest." And, as we do, our bodies and minds will be refreshed.

Never has rest been more important. We move at too fast a pace! Our adrenaline spigot is seldom shut off. As we race for late-night flights and add early-morning meetings, we are stretched beyond our limits. High adrenaline output depletes the brain's natural tranquilizers and sets the stage for high anxiety. Many of us have been trained to associate relaxation with irresponsibility, so some rewiring is needed.

Try this:

- *Don't overdo it.* Understand your limits.

If you think you have no limits, then you have more than most people.

- *Once you have reached your limits, stop.* Don't work until you drop. Find a pace of life that works for you, and stick to it.
- *Maintain regular breaks during the day.* Naps are biblical.
- *Give your mind a rest from technology.* Turn off, unplug, detach from social media, news, and all the tech toys that deplete energy.
- *Learn to relax.* To relax is to disengage and let go. An hour or daylong Sabbath is not the time to catch up with your work. It is a time to entrust your work to God. After all, he worked for six days and then rested. The world didn't fall apart. It won't for you either.

VERSE FOR REFLECTION

Come to Me, all you who labor and are heavy laden, and I will give you rest. Take My yoke upon you and learn from Me, for I am gentle and lowly in heart, and you will find rest for your souls. For My yoke is easy and My burden is light. (Matt. 11:28–30)

Pray It Through

Lord,

Break me of the need to be busy pursuing a sense of self-worth. Make me secure in who you are and who you have made me to be, and as a result, teach me what it means to truly rest.

In your holy name, amen.

Week 6

PRAY IT THROUGH

Worry is the interest we pay on the prayer-less life. Worry happens when we keep our problems to ourselves or present our problems to the puny deities of money, muscle, or humankind.

Peace happens when we pray. The act of prayer moves us from a spirit of concern to a spirit of gratitude. Even before our prayers are answered, our hearts begin to change. So take these steps:

- *Take your worries to God.* Set aside some time each day to pour out your concerns, complaints, fears, and woes to him. Tell him what is keeping you awake. Don't suppress; express! If you find yourself worrying about something during the day, write it down so you can bring it up in your next prayer session. Take everything to God and then . . . leave it with him. When the intrusive thought reenters your mind, remind yourself, *I left that one with God.*

- *Find a promise to match your problem.* When Moses prayed for the wayward Israelites, he sought God's favor, reminding God of what he had promised: "Remember Abraham, Isaac, and Israel, Your servants, to whom You swore by Your own self" (Ex. 32:13). Moses prayed for God's will based on God's Word.

- *Pray specifically.* Tell God exactly what troubles you so that when he answers the prayer, you will know.

VERSE FOR REFLECTION

Let us therefore come boldly to the throne of grace, that we may obtain mercy and find grace to help in time of need. (Heb. 4:16)

PRAY IT THROUGH

Almighty God,

Bolster my prayer life! Make me persistent, coura-geous, and specific. May I depend on communion with you as much as I depend on the air that I breathe. Teach me a little more each day what it looks like to "pray without ceasing."

In your Son's name, amen.

Week 7

GROW IN GRATITUDE

How positive or negative is your thinking? Try this exercise:

1. Take a few moments to sit and look around you.
2. Find something negative in everything you see.
3. Make a list of all the critical and unhappy thoughts that come into your mind.
4. Notice how you feel when you are finished, and write those feelings down.

Not much fun? A steady diet of critical, negative, and ungrateful thoughts leaves us critical, negative, and ungrateful. Now try the opposite approach.

1. Take a few moments and look around you.
2. Find something positive in everything you see.
3. Make a list of all the kind, generous, and grateful thoughts that come into your mind.
4. Notice the difference.

What if this exercise became a way of life? It can. Nobody other than you has the power to make you miserable and unhappy. As you pass through your day, look for opportunities to see the good in the world, in nature, and in life. This simple exercise will place your mind in a healthy posture of gratitude.

Verse for Reflection

Rejoice always, pray without ceasing, in everything give thanks; for this is the will of God in Christ Jesus for you. (1 Thess. 5:16–18)

Pray It Through

Lord,

I desire to be characterized by gratitude. I admit that I am more prone to dwell on the negative than the positive and to pine after the what-ifs rather than bask in the "alreadys." Give me the grace to truly rejoice in the many good gifts you have given.

In your holy name, amen.

Week 8

LEARN THE MESSAGE OF THE MANNA

God promised to supply Moses and the Hebrews with manna each day. But he told them to collect only one day's supply at a time. Those who disobeyed and collected enough for two days found themselves with rotten manna. The only exception to the rule was the day prior to the Sabbath. On Friday they could gather twice as much. In other words, God gave them what they needed in their time of need. "Give your entire attention to what God is doing right now, and don't get worked up about what may or may not happen tomorrow. God will help you deal with whatever hard things come up when the time comes" (Matt. 6:34 THE MESSAGE).

Doesn't each day have its share of challenges? Some of them repeat themselves over time; others are one-day specials. The key to tranquility is to face today's problems and no more, to treat each day like a self-contained unit. Here are today's problems. Meet them with God's strength. But don't start tackling tomorrow's problems until tomorrow. You do not have tomorrow's strength yet. You simply have enough for today. You can't cross a bridge until you reach it.

- *Find a parking place for tomorrow's problems.* When they surface, write them down and mentally drive them into a parking garage and leave them there.
- *Don't overstress your coping skills.* Emotional energy is finite. Give yourself permission to say, "I will solve

this tomorrow. By sunrise I will be replenished physically and mentally. Every day is a fresh start, so I will start fresh in the morning."

- *Shut the gate on yesterday, and don't touch the gate on tomorrow.* "This is the day the LORD has made; we will rejoice and be glad in it" (Ps. 118:24). You no longer have yesterday. You do not yet have tomorrow. You only have today. Live in it!

Consider the words of George MacDonald:

No man ever sank under the burden of the day. It's when tomorrow's burden is added to the burden of today that the weight is more than a man can bear. Never load yourselves so, my friends. If you find yourselves so loaded, at least remember this: it is your own doing, not God's. He begs you to leave the future to Him and to mind the present.[1]

Verse for Reflection

But seek first the kingdom of God and His righteousness, and all these things shall be added to you. Therefore do not worry about tomorrow, for tomorrow will worry about its own things. Sufficient for the day is its own trouble. (Matt. 6:33–34)

Pray It Through

Lord,

Thank you for the gift of another day of life! I praise you in advance for all that it holds. I give you the worries, anxieties, and fears that I am experiencing now and those that are yet to come. Carry them for me, and keep my focus on seeking your kingdom in every interaction and duty that confronts me today.

In Jesus' name, amen.

Week 9

TAKE RESPONSIBILITY
FOR YOUR FEELINGS

The boss put me in a bad mood. No he didn't. You put yourself in a bad mood.

This situation has me frazzled and out of sorts. No it hasn't. You've let the situation pull you down.

The kids are making me irritable. They may be misbehaving, but no one can make you irritable without your permission.

Peace 101 says that God is greater than your challenges. You are no one's victim. You are no one's pawn. In spite of a world gone wacko, you can remain at peace. Miss this truth, and you open the door to anxiety. If your peace is contingent on circumstances, you open the door to a horde of anxieties. Being happy is a choice. It's something you teach yourself to be.

Your peace does not depend on people, which is good, because they are fickle. Your peace does not depend on the government, which is good, because rulers come and go. Your peace does not even depend on a peaceful home; this is good, because kids tend to misbehave. Peace—long-lasting peace—depends on God.

With Jesus Christ living within you by the power of his Holy Spirit, you can take control of your thoughts before they take control of you. Remember, "the Spirit who lives in you is greater than the spirit who lives in the world" (1 John 4:4 NLT).

VERSE FOR REFLECTION

Peace I leave with you, My peace I give to you; not as the world gives do I give to you. Let not your heart be troubled, neither let it be afraid. (John 14:27)

Pray It Through

Lord,

I confess that I have chosen worry instead of peace. I have chosen irritation rather than calm. Time after time I give into my flesh rather than renounce it. Have mercy on my weary heart. By your Spirit give me the strength to abide in you rather than dwell on my earthly circumstances. Remind me today that my inner peace does not depend on temporal situations or fickle people but on you, my unchanging and loving Father.

In your name, amen.

Week 10

INTERRUPT THE
DOWNWARD SPIRAL

Anxiety is an out-of-control thought pattern. It settles over the mind like a severe weather system, spewing thunderclouds and casting lightning bolts. Life feels out of control, like an airplane in a tailspin. It feeds on what-ifs and worst-case scenarios. *What if the ankle is broken? What if insurance doesn't cover the treatment? I'll be laid up for weeks! They'll promote that kid to my job! I'll lose my paycheck. How will I survive on unemployment?* Down. Down. Down. Don't give in to this thought pattern. It's a sinkhole. Don't catastrophize your way into quicksand. Take a deep breath and then . . .

1. *Pray about it.* At the first hint of an anxious thought, pray. Take the thought captive. Don't tolerate the devil, not even for a second. Lasso the anxious thought with a word of prayer. *Lord, there is an intruder at the door! Please take over!*

2. *Identify the culprit.* Generalities are not permitted. None of this: "I'm worried." Get specific: *Lord, I'm worried about the layoffs at work.* Now, that's better. But even more detailed: *I'm worried that I will lose my job. Will I be able to find more work? Will we have to move?* Specificity disarms anxiety.

3. *Take a reality check.* Is this a legitimate concern? Is the company really laying off people? Do you know people who have lost their jobs? Or is this a vague, ill-defined, rumor-fed possibility? *They say layoffs are inevitable.* Who are *they*?

4. *Take an action step.* Assuming the concern is legitimate, what can you do? Make a list of two or three steps you can take. Resist the urge to try to solve everything immediately.

5. *Ask, "Can God solve this?"* Is this challenge within his skill set? Is he overwhelmed by this setback? Are the angels pounding on the door of heaven trying to convince him to come out of hiding? Is he resisting? *I can't handle Max's problem. It is too great. I don't know what to do! I'm stumped, stuck, and stalled out.*

I don't think so either. God is never baffled or belittled. Take the problem to him.

VERSE FOR REFLECTION

"No weapon formed against you shall prosper,
And every tongue which rises against you in
    judgment
You shall condemn.

This is the heritage of the servants of the LORD,
And their righteousness is from Me,"
Says the LORD. (Isa. 54:17)

PRAY IT THROUGH

Lord,

Thank you that "before a word is on my tongue you, LORD, know it completely" (Ps. 139:4 NIV). Thank you that there are no surprises with you. Help me find deep comfort in the fact that you are unshockable, and nothing is too great, too terrible, too large, or too heavy for you. Help me see the problems that face me today in light of how big you are. May I learn to trust you more and myself less.

Amen.

Week 11

TELL YOURSELF
THE TRUTH

The first word on the apostle Paul's medi-
tation list is *true*. One wonders if that
single word would have been enough. How
much energy is wasted on counterfeit concerns? Equip yourself with sleuthlike skills to
sniff out the truth.

- *Gather the facts.* How many planes
  actually fall out of the sky? How many
  bridges actually collapse? How many
  people die from the disease you dread?
  Examine the record. What are the odds

that the thing you are worrying about will ever occur?

- *Control what you can control.* Once you know precisely the challenge that faces you, make a list of what you can do about it. Do not indulge a drop of dread over matters beyond your control. Weather? You can't control it. (But you can watch the forecast.) The economy? You can't control it. (But you can keep a budget and live within your means.) Your boss's opinion of you? You can't control it. (But you can influence it by doing your work and not worrying about everyone else's.)

- *Don't second-guess yourself.* It does no good to do so. Make the best decision you can with the facts at hand, and live with it. Pray and take the next step.

VERSE FOR REFLECTION

Trust in the LORD with all your heart,
And lean not on your own understanding;
In all your ways acknowledge Him,
And He shall direct your paths. (Prov. 3:5–6)

PRAY IT THROUGH

Lord,

May my mind be so filled with truth that there is no longer any room for counterfeit concerns! May I both trust and listen as your Spirit guides me to what is true, good, and beautiful. Help me resist indulging in dread that is beyond my control. Teach me to rely on your guidance as I seek to be vigilant about my thought life.

In your precious name, amen.

NOTES

INTRODUCTION
1. *Haole* (pronounced HOW-leh) is a Hawaiian
   word for nonnatives, particularly white
   people. One definition comes from *ha*,
   meaning "breath" or "spirit," and *ole*,
   meaning "none" or "without." Some believe
   the term originated when the Christian
   missionaries first came to the islands.
   (Kapehu Retreat House, Hawaiian Words,
   www.kapehu.com/hawaiian-words.html).
2. Edmund J. Bourne, *The Anxiety and Phobia
   Workbook*, 5th ed. (Oakland, CA: New
   Harbinger, 2010), xi.
3. Taylor Clark, "It's Not the Job Market:
   The Three Real Reasons Why Americans
   Are More Anxious Than Ever Before," Slate,

January 31, 2011, http://www.slate.com
/articles/arts/culturebox/2011/01/its_not_the
_job_market.html.

4. Ibid.

5. John Ortberg, *Soulkeeping: Caring for the
Most Important Part of You* (Grand Rapids,
MI: Zondervan, 2014), 46.

6. Clark, "It's Not the Job Market."

7. Ibid.

8. Robert L. Leahy, *Anxiety Free: Unravel Your
Fears Before They Unravel You* (Carlsbad, CA:
Hay House, 2009), 4.

9. Bourne, *The Anxiety and Phobia Workbook*, xi.

10. Joel J. Miller, "The Secret Behind the
Bible's Most Highlighted Verse," *Theology
That Sticks* (blog), August 24, 2015,
https://blogs.ancientfaith.com/joeljmiller
/bibles-most-highlighted-verse/.

WEEK 8

1. George MacDonald, *Annals of a Quiet
Neighborhood* (Philadelphia: David McKay,
n.d.), 203. As quoted by Linda Dillow, *Calm
My Anxious Heart* (Colorado Springs, CO:
NavPress, 2007), 135.

Take the Next Step to Win the War on Worry

ISBN: 978-0-7180-9612-0
$22.99

Invite God to reframe the way you face your worries and fears. By his power you will "be anxious for nothing" and experience the "peace of God, which surpasses all understanding."

Available wherever books are sold.
AnxiousForNothingBook.com